I Remember

Pheasey

We'd got no library, no shops, no church, honest it was beautiful though, it was all fields.

This is the second in a series of *I Remember* booklets using oral evidence to look at various aspects of life that have now changed.

Pheasey's own story is that of farmland which became a thriving community and is recalled in the words of those who lived there and experienced the growth and development of their area first-hand.

Walsall
Leisure for all

ISBN 0 946652 33 3

Researched and edited by Joyce Hammond

Published by Walsall Metropolitan Borough Council
Walsall Local History Centre

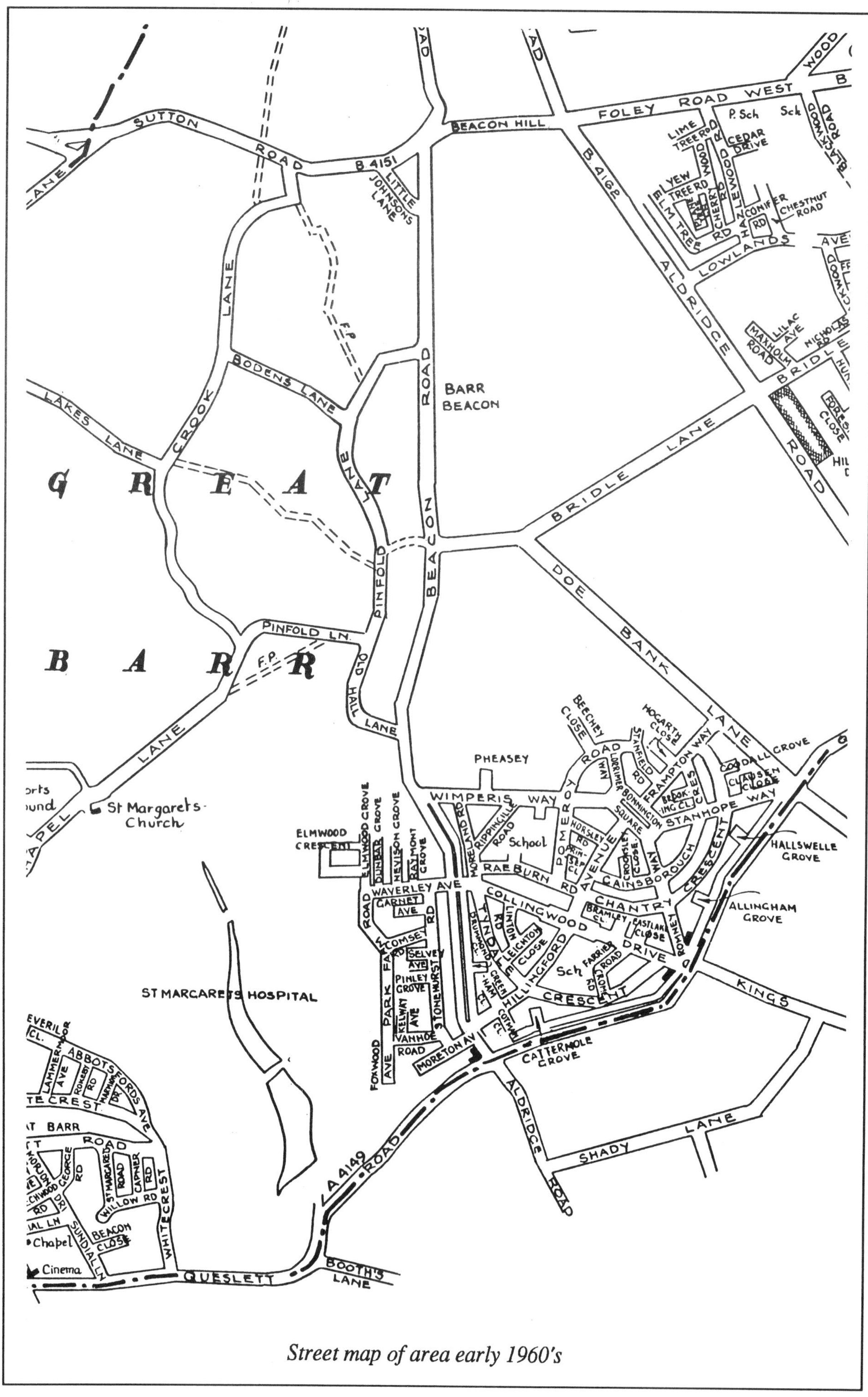

Street map of area early 1960's

Introduction

Today Pheasey is a large community on the southern side of Barr Beacon, spreading down to the Walsall boundary with neighbouring Birmingham. Pheasey Estate was started in the late 1930's on land belonging to the former Pheasey Farm; the adjacent Park Farm Estate was sold for development later, in 1955. However, it is the history of the former area that has been of chief interest for this booklet.

As the history of this community is in living memory, it has been possible to gather information from many residents who have witnessed the growth of Pheasey first-hand and who were willing to have their recollections preserved in tape recordings. Also, many newspaper articles, photographs, maps, archives, school records and printed sources have been used to draw together the history of Pheasey and enrich our understanding of the area.

The booklet does not claim to have covered all aspects of life here, but every attempt has been made to convey the spirit of those, mainly from Birmingham, building together their community on former farmland well away from the amenities of the city. The editors have tried to ensure that nothing obviously misremembered has been included without correction; our aim has been to preserve impressions of life there, and these, we are confident, can transcend any minor factual slips that they may contain.

I am indebted to the following people who have either contributed their own memories or who have told me of others who have subsequently done so and also to those who, when hearing of my interest in Pheasey, gave me the benefit of their own special knowledge.

Ronald Crisp
Mrs. Rachel Barton
Mrs. Marion Williams
Mrs. Janet Fry
Henry Fry
Mrs. Florence Wright
Mrs. Phyllis Baker
William Cornforth
Mrs. Olive Cornforth
Martin Collins
Herbert Keates
Leslie Hinsull
Councillor Bill Newman
Bob Reid
Rev'd Mary Stokes
Peter Allen
Alfred Goode
Frank Hudman
Gordon Baker

Background

Pheasey Farm was sold for housing development in 1935 by George Smith who had farmed the land since 1902. However, its history can be traced to 1559 and to land on the southern side of Barr Beacon known as Barr Lea. In that year a Simon Veysie purchased from one John Reddell a dwelling house, garden and orchard together with 80 acres of arable land, 12 acres of meadow, 30 acres of pasture and 40 acres of furze. He paid £80 for the land and property and it was this Simon Veysie who gave his name to the area later known as Pheasey farm.

The farm at Barr Lea soon passed into the possession of a branch of the Scott family and John Scott, who was rector at Great Barr between 1578 and 1622, farmed his own church land and also the farm at Barr Lea. He was an Oxford scholar and apparently a better lawyer than preacher. He prepared numerous wills for people at Great Barr and Aldridge and died a wealthy man. In 1648 the farm was given to Elizabeth Birch when she married Richard the second son of William Scott the elder of Great Barr. It would have been her source of income if she were left a widow.

Towards the end of the 18th century a young girl named Mary Anne Galton lived for a while with her parents at nearby Barr Hall, which had been leased from a member of the Scott family. When writing her autobiography some years later she described some of the scenery around Barr Beacon at this time. The area was renowned for its large flocks of black-faced sheep and she recalled there was a wide hilly common with a sheep path which led to the ancient manor house of Barr belonging to Mr. Scott's uncle, a Mr. Hoo, which was close by.

> This was one of those old-fashioned houses in which dark oak timber alternates with the lighter colour and material of the house itself; with oriel windows[1] and gable ends and bartizans[2]. Around it was an old-fashioned Dutch garden, full of fish-ponds. In the garden stood a yew tree, the branches extending about thirty-six yards round, which Dr. Plot, nearly 150 years ago, celebrated in his 'History of Staffordshire' as the largest in England.

[1] *supported on brackets or corbels*
[2] *parapet*

Close to the house were the kennels and she remembered seeing the hounds, huntsmen and gentlemen riding out and also hearing the hounds in full cry after their prey. On the summit of the Beacon was a group of old Scotch firs and a flag-pole erected by Mr. Scott upon which he ordered a flag to be flown on days he was receiving company and on all public occasions when a cannon was also fired to great effect.

A military exercise was carried out on Barr Beacon in September 1799 when the presentation of the standard and colours to the Walsall Volunteer Cavalry and Infantry took place. The day was described as fine and the spectators numerous.

> The Corps having passed the tents in review, went through their different manoeuvres and evolutions with great correctness. The attack and defence at speed of the cavalry, and close fire of the infantry, were particularly good ... The ground was kept by the Birmingham, Handsworth and Wolverhampton Cavalry, who afterwards attended the Corps into Walsall, where a grand entertainment was given by the Mayor and Corporation to their volunteers; and the day was spent and closed in the utmost harmony and conviviality.

In the summer of the following year Barr Beacon was occupied by a detachment of Royal Engineers who used the vantage point of the hill to make note of various bearings, angles, distances and features for the government survey of the countryside that was then being undertaken - The Ordnance Survey.

N-E VIEW of BARR CHAPEL.

To JOSEPH SCOTT, Esq. this View of the OLD HOUSE at BAR, &c. is inscribed, by his obliged servant. S. Shaw

Illustrations from History and Antiquities of Staffordshire c1800

Some years later, well known local historian Billy Meikle wrote in his memoirs that he had visited Barr Beacon area five times during his life. The first time was in 1869 when as a young art student he had sketched the Old Hall. He returned again in 1887 and 1897 when bonfires were lit in celebration of Queen Victoria's Jubilees. On the latter occasion he recalled how he had observed lights from the neighbouring beacons of Sedgley, Wrekin and Malvern and also the Walsall searchlight, which had been erected on a platform on the roof of the Police Station. Another memorable visit made by him was on Easter Monday 21 April 1919, when Barr Beacon was presented to the public in a ceremony attended by dignitaries from surrounding local authorities. The gift of the Beacon and surrounding land comprised about 150 acres and was from Colonel Wilkinson for the benefit of the people in perpetuity. A small area on the summit was set aside for a permanent memorial to the memory of those from Staffordshire and Warwickshire who gave their lives in the First World War. The weather on the day of the ceremony was excellent, the crowds were large, people had arrived in motor cars, motor buses and bikes and Meikle remarked how it was impossible to get close enough to hear any of the speakers.

Opening of Barr Beacon, 21st April 1919

In 1933 the way from Sutton Road to the Horns Inn at Queslett was named Beacon Road and in 1934 Pheasey Farm along with the rest of the area became part of the newly created Aldridge UDC. The area was rural with several farms scattered around the sides of the hill. Links with the towns were not easy, there was no convenient railway close by and considering it was only six miles from the centre of Birmingham and even closer to Walsall and Aldridge the bus service was very poor. Buses ran from Walsall via the Beacon to Streetly and to Kingstanding from Birmingham but at this time there was no regular through service. It wasn't until 1948 that a joint service was provided by Walsall and West Bromwich Corporation linking Scott Arms, Barr Beacon and Aldridge.

Farmland to Community

Pheasey Farm had belonged to the Scott family from the 17th century and was one of the properties arranged to be sold by auction in July 1921 with some other parts of the Great Barr Estate. However, it was withdrawn on the day of sale, presumably as an offer to purchase the farm had been made by George Smith, a tenant farmer here since 1902.

The two storey farmhouse was a mid 19th century replacement for a much earlier building and was surrounded by the usual outbuildings associated with a working farm. It was an arable farm with corn and vegetables grown. During the First World War many acres were used for potatoes and this crop continued to be grown successfully here afterwards.

In the 1930's First National Housing Trust, a subsidiary of Henry Boot & Sons Ltd., Sheffield, claimed to have received over 7,000 applications for houses on estates in Birmingham and that two thirds of these had been vetted by the Company and found suitable. At this time applications were being received at a rate of 90-100 a week, so another large estate was called for and apparently there was no suitable site available in the City.

In 1935 George Smith sold Pheasey Farm for a housing development to First National Housing Trust. They purchased 303,203 acres, all lying in Aldridge UDC with the exception of a small portion on the South side of Queslett Road which was within the City of Birmingham. They planned to build 4,225 houses and these were to be let almost entirely to people from Birmingham.

Pheasey Farm, 1937

It was planned to have 9½ miles of internal roads with shops, cinema, community centre and also sites were allocated for two schools at opposite corners of the estate. The houses were to be in semi-detached pairs, and blocks of four and six with rooms slightly larger than those on Perry Beeches Estate. It was estimated that 55,000,000 bricks and 25,000 tons of cement would be used. However, Aldridge UDC refused planning permission on the grounds that the density figures of twelve houses to an acre were not acceptable and also that there was not enough land reserved for an open space. Aldridge UDC recommended a density maximum varying from three to six houses per acre and 150 acres be kept as an open space. Aldridge claimed it was a very beautiful place, the land being undulating in character with belts of woodland that should be preserved. E. Boot, a director of the Trust, commented on the density recommended by Aldridge and claimed it would mean building a different class of house for which they would not get purchasers and therefore be unable to meet the demand for working class houses which was their aim.

In May 1936 an enquiry was held following an appeal by First National Housing Trust. The Trust representative claimed they could not develop the site economically with the suggested housing density and open space and claimed their plans had been satisfactorily used on other estates. However, the decision to refuse planning permission was overturned possibly due to the great demand for houses by Birmingham people. Mr. Boot in a statement in the Birmingham Post in July 1937 said that Aldridge UDC did not readily welcome the scheme and saw it as an incursion into an area they had hoped to keep as 'green belt'. When they realised the 'overflow' was inevitable they had been most helpful. An area of 68 acres was purchased from the Trust by Aldridge UDC which they intended to keep as an open space. The first house was to be ready in six months and it planned to have the whole scheme completed in three years.

The first sod was ceremonially cut on 13th July 1937 by the Minister of Health, Sir Kingsley Wood, using a chromium plated spade. In his speech he applauded the scheme for providing a number of houses with low rateable value that were being built by a private firm for letting and he congratulated First National Housing Trust on their enterprise.

All those interested in renting a house on Pheasey had to visit the offices of the Trust on the Beeches Estate and see a Miss Smith. They were vetted as to their suitability and it appears that those who were honest and reliable with good reasons for needing a house were put onto the waiting list. There were many who failed the test, but it has not been possible to find out the exact criteria for approval. Following the outbreak of war in September 1939 many seemed anxious to move from Birmingham and when the bombing raids commenced the demand increased again.

MOVING OUT OF THE CITY - Choosing houses, in the words of those who lived there and experienced this change in their lifestyle.

> I worked at a firm called Wales Ltd., just off Broad Street in Oozells Street, which has now disappeared under the new Convention Centre. One of the fellows who worked in the department lived in Eastlake Close and when he knew that we were getting married said, you want to come up they are building some houses by us. Before we made an application I went to see him in Eastlake Close, I can always remember it, because none of the roads of course were made up, in those days the roads came last ... it started to thunder and lighten and that was the first impression we had of Pheasey.

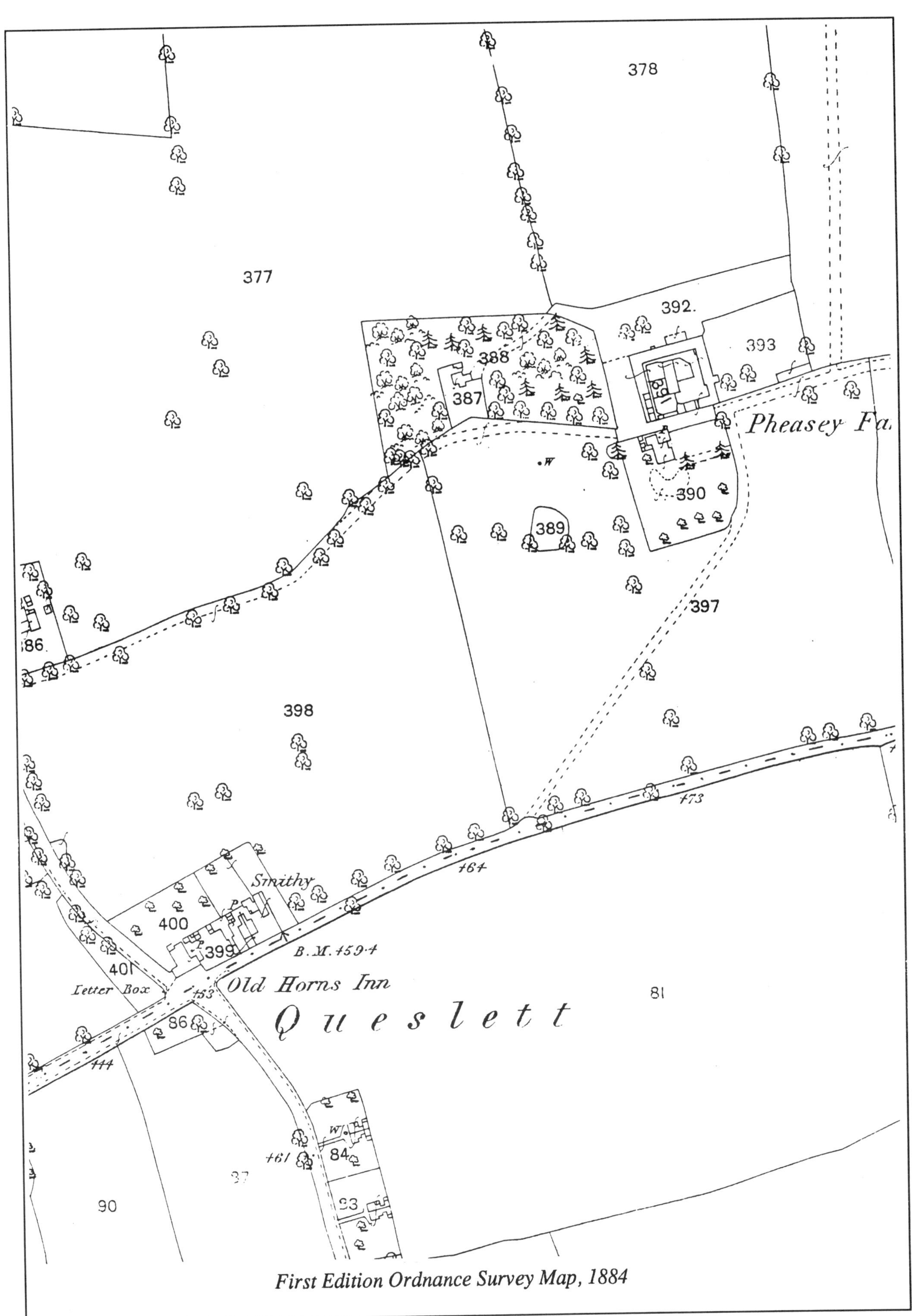

First Edition Ordnance Survey Map, 1884

We knew a war was in the offing, although when we first applied we never thought it would come to anything. ... We moved into the house the day war did break out, in the afternoon. The firm I worked for cancelled my weeks holiday so we had the day off on the Saturday to get married and then instead of having a honeymoon like from the Saturday for the following week I had to go back to work. The only thing we had forgotten was the blackout for the back so that was the first job we had to do the following week get some blackout stuff to put in; because even though this was a new estate there were wardens and that was the first time I heard 'put that light out!'.

When they told us that we could have a house my wife she wanted the walls to match her furniture. Miss Smith, [*of First National Housing Trust, and no relation to the Smiths of Pheasey Farm*] when you got to know her you were O.K. well here you are she said here's a list of twelve houses .. she gave us the numbers and we chose this one.

Q. She used to vet people before she would let them rent a property?

Oh yes, she didn't tell us what she was looking for, but obviously you passed the scrutiny O.K. I don't know how far away people did come but they must have come from all parts of Birmingham. Well I know they have come from Aston around there, Perry Barr way and so on.

I don't know the actual percentage but I would hazard a guess and say at least ninety five percent of the people who came to live at Pheasey were all couples the same as ourselves, young married couples without families. I don't ever remember youngsters, we had an older couple next door they'd got a son.

I was evacuated to Monmouth from Lozells and no-one knew where you were being sent to when you were evacuated you know.

Q. That was before you came here?

Yes, if you had got a baby twelve months you had to go whether you wanted to or not and there was me and another neighbour walking down that big main road to Monmouth and a motor bike went past and as he went past he shouted do you come from Birmingham? We shouted yes, and we all went running down the street carrying babies, and he came from the same place as we did, and we said our husbands don't know where we are. We said will you tell them when you go back and he said yes, and my husband came up the next weekend to see us on his motor bike. It was funny meeting somebody like that, you see everybody was moved out and you didn't know where you was going to land up. I didn't stop a fortnight because we had got this house, Miss Smith gave us this house and I came back, it was out of the danger area here you see. ...

On the Beeches estate, it was called the Whitehouse I don't think it is there now, I think it has all been pulled down, we had to see this lady, this Miss Smith and she said why do you want to leave and my husband said I think it's going to be a bit hectic in town and we would like to come a bit further out in the country, which it was then it was lovely country. Well, she said, you bring your rent books and all your bills and I will think about it and I will let you know. So we went the next weekend, took the rent book and

The Minister of Health (Sir Kingsley Wood) speaking at the formal inauguration of Pheasey Farm Housing Estate in July 1937. On the front row next to him is Mr. Boot Chairman of the building firm.

Farmland where Pheasey Estate now stands, mid 1930's

the bills and she looked at them and she said, oh you've done well haven't you. She was funny, but nice and fair. Anyway she said there are three lots of keys here, she said, go and pick your own house and she just let us pick our own house. And we had number 85.

It was not unknown for Miss Smith to visit the home of a prospective tenant or existing one if they wanted to exchange to another house belonging to the Trust.

[My husband] said when this house came to be let he said we'll go and see if we can exchange. So we went to see her *[Miss Smith]* she said well I will come and have a look at your house and let you know. So she came this one Friday and it would be about 12 o'clock when she came and I'd got it all nice and clean and the baby was in bed and the other kids was off at school. She came in and had a look and she said I'll go and have a look at that other lady's house and I'll let you know, I can't promise you anything. She was back in about five minutes and she said you can have it. I said are you sure? Yes I am, she said, she'd got cob-webs in her bedrooms and if she can't keep cobwebs out of a two bedroomed house, she can't keep them out of a three bedroomed house. And she gave it me then and she wouldn't let her have my house, she wouldn't let her exchange for my house.

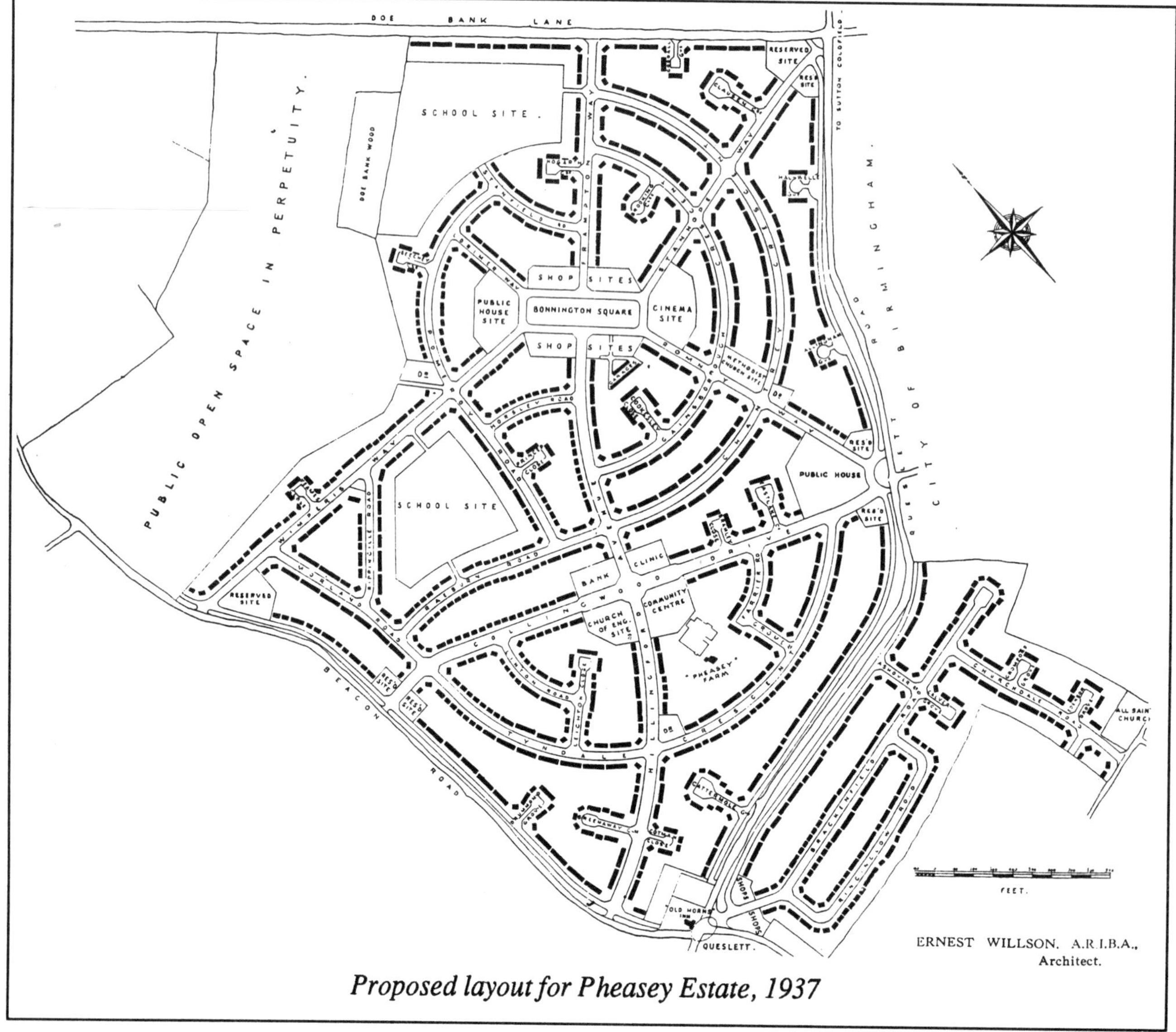

Proposed layout for Pheasey Estate, 1937

Q. She was very particular about who she let rent the houses?
Oh she was, she'd look in your bedclothes, well that's what she did, she said do you mind if I go upstairs and have a look and I knew she had pulled the bedclothes up 'cause I could tell and the baby was in his cot and she'd moved his bed and had a look in his cot and she'd come down and said nice and clean yes, lovely and clean. And that's how we come to live here.
Q. About what year would this have been?
About 1942.

My husband went and he came back with two keys ... So we looked at both these houses, one was a two bedroomed house at 11/5 a week the other one was 12/3 a week a three bedroomed house. So we had the three bedroomed house because it had got its own path up to the front door, we didn't share a path, we liked that so we had it. We came up here, all through the war years up here.
Q. So what was the house like inside, was the decorating done for you?
Oh it was all emulsion paint, if you wanted it decorating you had to decorate it yourself, it was all lovely and clean like a new house just finished you see, it wasn't papered then. It had got red quarries in the kitchen, the toilet and the coal house was as you come in the back door like you know. We opened the other door and there was the back kitchen with the sink in, the cooker and the wash boiler and then you went into the hall and you'd got the front room and three bedrooms upstairs and the bathroom.
Q. What sort of cooker did you have, was it a gas one?
A gas one, the cooker was already put into your house you didn't have to buy a cooker or a boiler to boil your washing in ... that was already in the house.
Q. Can you tell me what sort of furniture you had first of all?
Well there was my dining table and chairs - oak, and so was me sideboard. We hadn't got a radio, a wireless then, my mother-in-law gave us a radiogram a wind-up one, she had bought it for *[my husband]* so she said we could have it. She gave me his single bed and chest of drawers so that helped to fill up the little box room ... we added as we went on, we didn't have a three piece suite. I have got two chairs in the bedroom as I had when we first got married, in the front room, Cintique chairs.
Q. What about on the floor, carpets or rugs?
We had lino in the bedroom, carpet up the stairs, oh that was very nice. I used to polish the red cardinal tiles in the hall and have a hall runner, because you couldn't get the stuff during the war you see, unless you had the coupons anyway.
Q. How much garden did you have?
Oh quite a big garden, ... we had a greenhouse after the war he grew his own tomatoes and cucumbers and we used to dig it over and I put the vegetables in to grow and all the plants and things. As long as he dug it I'd plant it. ...

Newcomers to Pheasey in the early days felt cut-off from the bustle of city life and its amenities. There were one or two shops at Queslett and a few more at Kingstanding, but for anything out of the ordinary most people travelled into Birmingham and this meant a long walk to the nearest bus stop. The winter of 1940 was particularly severe and food shortages were beginning to cause hardships.

Houses being constructed, 1939

Q. How had you used to get to work from here, was there a bus service?
No, we had to walk from here down to Kingstanding Circle which was every bit I would say of at least three quarters of a mile and it was rough going. And we used to catch the bus from there to town back of Colmore Row, Newhall Street, and the trams used to go there then.

And another thing it was a terrible winter the first winter at the Christmas, first year of the war, the snow, we couldn't get any coal, we had to push prams down to the Horns to get coal and to get milk, the milkman couldn't come round. And you know Old Hall lane, the snow was right up to the top of the trees and we had an old man that used to come from up there to sweep the roads and he made a hole and he did in 1947 the same as 1939, he made a path just so that he could get through. They didn't put any felting under the tiles in these houses and that Christmas and in 1947, twenty buckets of snow we got out of our loft, everybody had the windows open throwing it through the bedroom windows.

The first winter we came up here it was a bad one and there was still one or two empty houses and people were coming in and of course when they put the fires on they found the pipes was burst, oh it was dreadful and folks had got no coal, 'cause the coal man couldn't get through the snow and we had to lend buckets of coal and folks hadn't got potatoes so we shared out potatoes. ... There was no Park Farm, no Co-op on that side, there was all fields along there except one little lodge house that a person used to live in and a drive way that used to go up to St. Margaret's, the hospital, and then there was no Cat and Fiddle and on the other side it was only a small hut, not a very big hut and that was the Co-op. *[opened in 1940]*.
I used to have me ration books at Wrensons, I used to walk all that way for my rations pushing a pram with two babies in it ... I used to have a big pram and there was a space underneath and I used to take the kiddies out and put me shopping in there and wheel them all the way back again. We were all fit, because there was no buses. We had to walk everywhere. We'd dig our gardens and when we first came up here we even dug the front up, dug the lawn up.
Q. What did you plant?
Potatoes and veggies and all that, and that helped us a lot. I'd got Kilner jars if there was any fruit going I would bottle fruit. We'd exchange things, if somebody had got a bit more sugar and didn't take so much sugar we'd swap, perhaps a jelly or half a jelly or a packet of blancmange powder and that's how we'd manage. Or if the butchers had got a queue you'd wonder what they were queuing up for, sausages, you'd go and join the queue and he'd give you about half a dozen sausages and that was wonderful that was. We managed, but there weren't many fat people about I can tell you that. ...

You had to walk down to the Circle to catch a bus to go to town ... or unless you went to Walsall and then that was worse still. There was no buses to go to Walsall you had got to walk up to the Scotts Arms and catch a bus. Well I mean you used to wear your shoes out and your shoes was on your clothing coupons, you had to be so careful.

> But you used to make do and mend. I had got a coat that had gone a bit shabby I had to unpick it turn it inside out and make a little coat for the little ones. ...When you think back, you think I never did that but you had to.

In the 1940's and 1950's the Beacon area still retained its rural character with farms still working the land. Milk was delivered from Wright's farm by horse and cart and this was ladled out of churns for customers. Every May Day the horse was trimmed up with ribbons plaited into his mane and tail.

> Over there I have seen the beagles come across right from Old Hall Lane right down to the Horns and we could see them and they'd come up there with the dogs, they weren't on horseback, with the beagles and I've seen the hare run right down to the bottom. It was lovely at night and there wasn't a light, I could look from my bedroom window, and after these two front rows of houses there was nothing, all dark, I used to think it was lovely...

A meet of the South Staffordshire Beagles, 1951

Ploughing on Park Farm, early 1950's

On the Beacon Road side from the cottages at the bottom of the road where the garage is, all as far back as St. Margaret's Hospital all that was beautiful corn. ... When it was out it was beautiful just like a sea of waves.
Oh they had the old fashioned combines then, not those modern things they have got today, but they did have a couple of horses. It was nearly all done by hand wasn't it. All the way up right from Hillingford Avenue, when the buses started to run at the top of Hillingford you could look straight down Collingwood Drive and you could see all the corn blowing in the wind. *[Park Farm was not sold for housing until 1955].* We used to go up to the farm in Doe Bank Lane, to Wright's farm and get eggs, I used to go across the fields and pick mushrooms on the way up, it was lovely.
You used to see the ducks flying over, the water hens, and I've seen swans fly over. There used to be quite a large pond at the back of Wright's farm down in the hollow, that's coming up Wimperis Way at the back of the houses there, but I think some of it has been filled in.
Q. Were there many people that didn't settle on the estate and moved away?
Well the people that really left went because there wasn't that many schools and there wasn't buses to get anywhere you know. I think that's the only reason they moved. I can't see any other reason because they all liked the houses. Or their husbands were killed during the war, and they moved to other areas or when the parents died, or the kids got married and they moved. I think everybody that knew Pheasey as it was couldn't say that they didn't like it.

The outbreak of war in 1939 seriously interrupted building progress and plans for the development of communal life on Pheasey. By that time about 1700 houses had been built, the estate was planned to hold 4,225 houses, and First National Housing Trust were prepared to accept responsibility for the social and cultural life of the residents. However, the completion of a Community Centre in Collingwood Drive, destined to be one of the finest in the country, was halted. A large barn at Pheasey Farm was offered to the newly formed Community Association as temporary accommodation and this was adapted into an assembly hall. Pheasey Farm complex was being used by the Trust as offices and workshops. The Barn, or Old Barn as it became fondly known, was in use every night for a variety of meetings, lectures, concerts, whist drives, dances and entertainments. On Sundays it was used as a place of worship. A branch of the Staffordshire County Library had been established and a Citizens Advice Bureau was started at the onset of war. Also a Comforts Fund Committee was set up which worked in co-operation with Aldridge UDC Comforts Fund to help men from the estate who were serving in the armed forces.
Henry Boot was the President and George Smith the Chairman of the Community Association and their main concerns at this time were lack of public transport and the fact that there was no school on the estate for the large number of children who now lived here. British and American troops were billeted in many of the new houses on Pheasey and the building intended as a show-piece community centre became their administrative and social headquarters.

The Old Barn Community Centre, early 1950's

PHEASEY'S OWN STORY CONTINUES ...

> Yes it was nearly completed as a Community Centre and then the forces come in and took over. ... We had the Pioneer Army first.
> Q. Did you have any problems with air raids?
> No we took precautions and blackouts but nothing ever happened here, we heard them go over. I know I was out with a friend going up to the Circle and we watched the Germans, 'cause you could tell the sound of the German planes, and we'd got our babies in a pram and we didn't know where to go, we stood just watching them, you could see them through the trees going over ...
>
> Over the road it was a four block and in the middle was an entry and they put blast walls up at the back and we'd all go in there for air raids.
> Q. Was this a separate wall they built?
> Yes, 'cause your entry was all open back and front and they put us a blast wall up and we took mattresses in and slept in there and we was always in and out of the entry. We'd go in different ones houses and make the tea until the all-clear went and then we'd go back home and go to bed again ...

Pheasey had its own platoon of the Home Guard and their headquarters were at The Trees public house.

> Mr. Small was the lieutenant, and we all lived round about. We had got alarm arrangements for invasion and every so often we would go to the tin church on Aldridge Road. We used to be on guard there about once a fortnight just a small group ... Somebody was on duty all night so we used to take it in turns we did it in shifts. In case of any bother or any parachutists or anything like that we had got rifles and ammunition and all the rest of it and we had to alarm all the other local platoons.

Life in Birmingham was beginning to get disrupted by enemy action.

> We were still in Roland Road, Handsworth ... and things started to happen, we had some pretty bad raids. The one big bomb which was a land mine, they dropped on a parachute, and the explosion spread out and it did a lot of destruction to buildings, it didn't go down in the ground and blow up, it spread out sideways. It battered our house pretty well, blew the doors in and all the windows were smashed and all the rest of it ... after the one raid which was a Friday night, this woman who my wife had been evacuated with was now living in Morland Road and she came down and suggested if we would like two or three nights rest from the raids, being up all night with air raids we could come up here and stop with her, which we did.
> It was so nice to get out of the raids and the bombing ... fire bombs and all the rest of it, we decided we would try and get a house. She said if you go down to the Whitehouse, which was on Beeches Road, you could have your name put down and when there comes a house available you've got the chance to have it. So we did that, we got someone to bring our furniture we left our house in Handsworth and came to live up here. We stored the furniture in various houses around, a bit here and a bit there. Her husband

had been called up, he was in the army, so there was my mother and father in law as well with us, their house was the same 'cause it was only three doors away, it had been damaged the same as ours. At this time the houses up Rippingille Road petered out about half way up 'cause they were still building and everything stopped. There were no houses on the right hand side of Morland Road nor the left hand side up Rippingille it was all grass fields in those days, and Wimperis Way was just a path from Beacon Road right the way up onto the other estate.

When the men escaped Dunkirk all sorts were evacuated and they were all mixed up and some were put into these houses until they could be sorted out and put back into the force again. So the people who were living in the houses, there were a few occupied, they moved them out and made a solid block of houses to keep as a camp. The first people to occupy them were all the battered remains of the army that had gone over to fight the Germans in France and escaped from Dunkirk. Well after that, I think the next lot of people that we saw were the Pioneers Corps, they came and they were part of the set up round here.

There are very many memories of the U.S. troops billeted here who were part of the 10th Replacement Unit based at Lichfield. At this time it was a new estate and many of the young people made good friends with those stationed here.

Pheasey was part and parcel of the Lichfield Area and this was what they called a transit camp at Pheasey which they developed and right throughout the war we literally had thousands of soldiers, American soldiers black and white coming here and the U.S.A. Army was situated in Collingwood Drive School. Their officers had quite a number of the houses in Eastlake Close and Bramley Close and towards where the library is now you see.

Q. Do you remember the forces moving in?

Oh yes, our houses used to come to the back where the forces were, 'cause they were in Rippingille which was at the back or our house. They put up a big wire and we used to pass odds and ends over the wire 'cause I used to do them a bit of washing. We had some lovely friends and they used to say are you going to do any chips? 'Cause they could smell when we had done chips. And I would say no, I haven't got any fat, I mean we only had a little bit of fat about a quarter of an ounce.

Well they said if we give you a bit of fat will you cook us some chips and I'd say if I've got enough potatoes I will and I'd done it once or twice and in the finish they got as they threw me a few potatoes over and I'd cook 'em the chips. I mean they was a long way from home and they was ever such nice kids.

Q. Did you feel sorry for them?

Oh yes 'cause they was only like my age and perhaps younger and me husband's age. Some of them was only about 17 or 18 you could tell. They'd say I've got ever such dirty shirts could you wash me shirts for me and I'd wash the shirts while I was doing me own washing and some would shout at the bottom of the garden can I have my shirts back and I'd say well they are not even dry and they'd say can't help it we are off. And I'd roll up the shirts and give 'em back, I don't know how they got on with them, whether they dried them going along I don't know.

... They were in the houses and then they built big huts which was like the dining things and the cookhouse and things like that. But I suppose they only had a certain amount of food the same as we did, and they couldn't go in the cookhouse if they fancied a few chips. It was a lovely time really the only thing was, you'd see 'em go and you'd think I wonder if they'll ever come back. I mean a lot of 'em didn't, they were the first to go abroad when they started to go into France and that.

And the first lot that come they knocked on your door and asked if you had got a spare room and a bed? Which we had, and they said could you put someone up? ... All of them with spare beds had to put somebody up. And we had a girl and we had her for about a fortnight and I think she'd have her breakfast and then she'd come home and have her evening meal and then bed. I think they paid us about 16 shillings a week for giving them a couple of meals and a bed. But 16 shillings in them days was a lot of money.

Q. Was she army or a nurse?

No just an army lady. I don't know what she did I didn't ask. 'Cause you couldn't ask questions or you couldn't ask where they were going or anything like that, wagging tongues. 'Cause they wouldn't tell you anyway. It was a bit of a problem because we didn't have any rations for that one, we had to give up part of our rations.

She was a nice person, but I don't know what happened to her when she left. ... We got to know such a lot, if any of them had got killed I would have been worried to death, so I was glad really I didn't know.

American Servicemen in a local pub, c1944

... and I remember they very often used to get lost and they'd come and knock the door, 'cause ours was the last house. There was a fish and chip shop down at the Old Horns they were very fond of and I used to lend them a flash lamp so they wouldn't get lost so they could find their way down there, and they always brought it back.
And, actually we invited two or three of them to come in when we got to know them and the one chap, he was very nice, Joe his name was, he came from Buffalo by Niagara Falls, they used to bring the lads chocolate and that sort of thing when they came and we'd give them what we'd got sort of thing and sometimes they would bring us other things from the PX as they called it, their NAAFI, and we made friends and wrote to their parents, the one chap's parents sent us a food parcel which was very useful, very nice, a luxury for us to have the things in it that they had sent.
When they left, the one came back one time and stayed with us over the weekend, when he was on his way home, we kept in touch for a while but we lost track in the end.
The ones we knew were here quite a while because we got friendly with them. We used to have a game of cards or whatever, talk you know, they'd show us things from their country. These people were a gun unit a hard track they called it, it moved like a caterpillar gun, quite a heavy thing ...

Q. Do you think other people were as friendly towards the American troops as you were when you tried to help them?
Yes, yes.
Q. I have come across some people who had almost been afraid to be too friendly towards them in case they got a name or reputation.
Oh, no, no I never looked at it like that, I was a young married woman with children I had got no time to even think about that. No, they were a long way from home and a lot of them missed their homes, no I didn't even think about it, no. I mean I used to have them come in the house and they would bring the kids a few sweets on the ration but very rare. I used to think, well they can come and have a warm by my fire any time for a few sweets for the kids. It was a shame really that they had to come all this way to fight.
Yes they had children's parties in the camp.
I think I remember on two occasions, the Home Guard organised concerts for the Americans who came through, in The Trees, that was our headquarters The Trees.

They were ever so good to the children during the war, they used to have a party at Christmas. We got the name because there was soldiers here. The buses had started by then, they used to call it the Pheasey special. Well the women came from Birmingham and of course a lot of us got the names and you was frightened to be too friendly with them and I know two people who used to go with them. But you know I never heard a wrong word from any of them, they were very kind. I remember coming along Beacon Road once and you know the hedges there, and there was a battalion walking up in front of me and there was no other way of getting up home, and I was walking up with the pram, and all of a sudden they fell out, a whole battalion and they all jumped out onto the edges all the way along and I had to come through the lot of them with the baby. And there wasn't a murmur, not a word at all, I was only thirty four and I felt very shy. Only when we got past one group and they saw my baby just peeping over the edge and they just said oh. It was ever so nice of them, but very embarrassing.

I was very sorry for these lads 'cause they were only lads and they were away from their own country and I saw one of them die. You know Queslett Road towards the Deers Leap on this side there was no houses then but they had got great big tents, but the soldiers that had come back from the war that had been in the fighting, the Americans came back there and they slept in these tents. And I was going up there once and I saw this chap collapse and in a minute there was doctors and men round him but he died. He just fell down and died, it upset me, I cried, I thought some poor mother is going to have a broken heart isn't she?...

One day I had got my second little boy in a pram and we were going out and my other boy who was four, he said, Mommy, he said, the Americans they are giving little boys balloons, can I have one? And I said I will buy you a balloon when we go out, so I put the baby in the pram and we went round the corner and as soon as we went round the corner he said, oh there's one of those balloons in the gutter, can I have it. Do you know you never talked about condoms in those days, I didn't know what they looked like but as I saw it I guessed what it was. Oh, I said you mustn't touch anything in the gutter, I will buy you a balloon, but when we got up to the school there weren't railings around the school then and all the soldiers were sitting all the way round and killing themselves laughing, they'd blown them up and put them on sticks to give to the kids. It was most embarrassing 'cause you had to go past them, they were killing themselves laughing.

However, not all welcomed the aspect of American troops living amongst them on the estate and some were unsure of their natural over friendly approaches. Ladies of easy virtue from outside the area were attracted to the U.S. camp and this gave a certain notoriety to Pheasey at this time and was generally disapproved of by residents.

You could never go out at night when they were about. I wouldn't go outside my door unless my husband was with me. ... It was not only me, if you went to the Circle to do your bit of shopping they would follow you all the way home. I went to my neighbours once and her husband was home he had come home from work, I said you have got an American in your front garden I said, he's followed me all the way from the Circle, he told him where to go. ... they were a right real lot I can tell you.

In the compound on the sandpits they were all in huts and they were billeted in these houses from the bottom of Hillingford Avenue to this corner here of Horseley they weren't completed, but they took over and they also moved people out ... they moved people that were already in paying rent out. They moved them into other areas into Pomeroy Road or Collingwood Drive so they could have all the unit into one. The houses, not these last few modern ones they built by the library 'cause that used to be grass like a continuation of where all the sandpits were. They fenced all that off but they had all the houses coming out of the two roads round the corner. The Trees was built

American servicemen in a local pub, c1944

of course, that had been completed, all the houses on that side of Collingwood all the way down to Beacon Road, they were all there.

Q. People have told me about the Pheasey Specials?

That was a nightmare I can tell you, going to work you'd get somebody come and plonk themselves down, been out all night, slept in their clothes you could tell they had, shocking. In the finish, they had the Military Police you know and the buses only used to run as far as the Trees, they didn't come up onto the estate and they used to stop you for your I.D. card your identification card and if you didn't live on the estate they'd turn them back. It got that bad, oh they stopped my husband and I many a night when we've come home on the bikes. They wouldn't let you go by unless you showed your I.D. card to prove that you lived on the estate.

I've seen Americans knock on the front door and go in and the husbands have come home from work and they've gone out the back, been there all night.

Q. Their part of the estate was completely fenced off?

Oh yes, they had got guards, M.P's and things like that. It was sort of like a clearing station, they would have them come from America and bring them here and wait for orders to ship 'em out. Some weren't here for long two or three weeks at the most and then they'd have a new lot come. ...

Q. There must have been a lot visited here over the war years then?

Oooh, ever such a lot. Until they started to invade and they got across to France and then they gradually dwindled down because they could send them straight to the coast you see, instead of bringing them here in the first place.

When you come to think way back, when the Yanks were here, it was only because the American soldiers or the powers that be in their forces decided that we started to have some street lights. Now when I tell you those lights were on the top of wooden poles they weren't the ordinary old type of street lighting that's what we had. A lot of the roads particularly the surface roads were not made up and we hadn't got a clinic then. ... The Yanks, having the school hall, they used to have a projector there and show films and they'd got in that school hall certainly the largest stage I would think of any theatre in and around the Midland area so much so that it was always said you could get six double decker buses on that stage. ... They were also instrumental in getting a bus service up here because way back towards the end of the war years we did start to have a bus come up here you see. Originally they moved it from the Circle down Kingstanding to Lambeth Road and then finally it was brought up here.

At the end of the war the remaining troops cleared out of the houses and areas they had occupied on Pheasey. The burning of bedding on waste land near to The Trees public house was recalled by someone living near at the time.

The Americans also burned new bedding and mattresses near the Trees public house, when people complained that we were unable to purchase such items they were told it was so as not to upset the economy locally. I was 16 at that time so I suppose I didn't retain much in my memory except 3 pence bought a packet of 20 Camel cigarettes, and some of my mates dressed up in what's now known as drag to scrounge stuff. There used to be a pub called the King Charles in Kings Road where I saw heaps of fights between G.I.'s and our soldiers, particularly at the time of Arnhem battle.

I only very vaguely remember any Americans, it was 'have you got any gum chum' that was a statement you know I can remember saying that as a youngster with a group of other kids.

Q. When they left, did they have a farewell party?
No, they just quietly went and all the houses were refurbished, they reckon a lot of them were knocked about a lot.
When they had gone there was no banisters or anything left they had chopped them down. Anything that was wood they chopped down to make a fire. There wasn't much furniture or stuff in.
They had got bunk beds, like two or three to a room, I went in one time, a couple of chairs very, very sparse it was.

Q. What were the celebrations like at the end of the war, street parties?
Oh we had street parties galore we did, we had a great big marquee on where the Americans had cleared off, a lot of grass had grown so they had a great big marquee on the grass, all the way down Hillingford different groups of parties and flags were out you know and all the kids they had a whale of a time and we did as well.
We had a bonfire in the street and by the time it had gone out we had got a hole in the road, I can't ever remember what happened to that hole but they must have filled it in ... and somebody bought a piano out, I don't know

VJ Party in the Old Barn, 1945

> whose piano it was. We'd got a piano in the street. It went on nearly all day and half the night till we got too tired to carry on.

After the war the houses that had been occupied by the American troops were offered for sale and the demand for those was considerable with reports of long queues of interested people outside the office of the Trust anxious to buy homes for prices of between £500-£575 each.

> The houses used by the British and American troops were put up for sale. We came and looked at them, but had doubts about purchasing as they were in a bad state. Most of the woodwork had been used for fuel in the hard winters during the war and not painted in all those years. They had no interior walls upstairs yet were structurally quite sound. We were assured by Boot's management that they would be completely refurbished and this promise was fully kept.

> This was just a wood *[Frampton Way]* believe it or not and the only signs *[of the Americans]* was what was left up here. It was right on the top of the hill and it was a wood the nearest house was down Hillingford, which is across the junction here. There was the police house which is on the left hand side to Hillingford just past the cross roads here and they are still there today, but not as police houses. They stood on their own just across the road from us here is the sub-station and that was there from as far back as I can remember right in the middle of the woods. The trees, you can actually see some of the trees they are obviously the original trees but around the back here must have been slip trenches parts of air-raid shelters and we used to play in them as youngsters. We used to come up to the woods, it was a great adventure.

Social Activities in the Old Barn

MONDAY:
6.0—8.30—Kiddies' Kinema
8.30—10.30—Dramatic Society.
8.30—10.30 — Assoc. Whist Drive (W. Fulleylove, Sen.)

TUESDAY:
6.0—8.30—Kiddies' Kinema
8.30—10.30—Adults' Cinema
8.0—British Legion.

WEDNESDAY:
6.30—8.0—Wolf Cubs (W. Smith).
8.0—10.30—Assoc. Dance.

THURSDAY:
6.30—8.15—Scouts (D. Parker).

THURSDAY (cont'd):
8.15—10.30—Concert Party (R. Cure).
8.0—Chess Club.

FRIDAY:
7.30—9.0—Sick & Dividend Club (W. G. Roberts).
8.0—10.0—Indoor Games (W. A. Clarke).
8.0—10.30—Garden Guild (W. E. Piper).

SATURDAY:
2.30—5.0 — Children's Dancing Class (Miss J. Grey).
8.0—10.30—Assoc. Activities

Poultry Club: First Tuesday and last Wednesday each month, 8.15 p.m.
Billiards, Snooker and Darts may be played every night except Sunday.

Outdoor Activities:
FOOTBALL *(Sec.:* J. Greaves) CRICKET *(Sec.:* A. Adey)

GROWING UP AT PHEASEY

A report appeared in the Walsall Observer in November 1940 stating that Staffordshire Education Committee were taking steps to deal with the problem of 300 children on Pheasey Estate who were being deprived of an education. It had been hoped to build a school on the estate and provisional plans had been drawn up, but postponed due to wartime restrictions on building. The children were to be transported instead to and from schools in Pelsall and Rushall.

The school log books at Pheasey Infants School in Wimperis Way have some interesting details about the early years of their school.

13 April 1942	Temporary school opened.
7 April 1943	A fierce gale today, this morning 2 doors jammed and the roofs are in danger of loosing the waterproof felting.
18 April 1944	U.S. Army Concert Party gave a concert for school funds, £11.0.0. was raised which will purchase a gramophone.
21 July 1944	A special holiday for reaching the target in the Salute a Soldier campaign.
8 June 1945	Major Winston U.S.A. Commanding Officer came to say goodbye before remainder of the U.S. forces stationed at Pheasey left. He gave chairs and tables to the teachers.
23 July 1946	Mr. Woodall came to school to discuss the new proposals re the Community Centre.
24 July 1946	Staff were disappointed with the proposals.
26 July 1946	We shall remain in the huts, but improvements have been promised. Children who reach 7 on 1st September next will leave on Wednesday 31 July and attend the new Junior School, to be called Community Centre Temporary School.
25 Oct 1948	Raeburn Road entrance to school was officially closed today. The new school is to be built.
16 June 1950	The old school will be closed tonight.
21 Sept 1950	School will be officially opened tonight by Mr. Alderman Lewis Davies, the Chairman of Staffordshire C.C.

Pheasey's new school was floodlit for its official opening and was described by the press as a 'Palace on the Hill' due to the 'clean cut elegance of its buildings and magnificently equipped interior'. The school accommodated 440 children when it opened and planned to have places for 920 children when completed. At this time it was the largest school in the authority's post war programme. The building in Collingwood Drive, planned as a Community Centre before the war and requisitioned by the army, was obtained in 1946 by the L.E.A. to provide accommodation for a Junior School.

So children who began their education in temporary classrooms were now being taught in probably one of the best schools in the area. When Raeburn Road School was finally completed and both infants and juniors established there, Collingwood Drive School became a senior school. However, as the demand for schools in the area was increasing a new Barr Beacon School opened in Old Hall Lane in 1958 and also Doe Bank School in 1964.

'Cause there was no school when we first come up here. They used to catch a bus at the bottom of Collingwood Drive, the kiddies who were old enough to go to school and they used to go to Pelsall and the bus would bring 'em back again.

Evangelical youth rally on Barr Beacon, 1958

I've always been to school on the estate, the first school was a sort of Primary School which is now part of Raeburn Road Schools. ... Wimperis Way was the way we got to it and they moved us for a while up to Collingwood Drive, which was the Junior School then, while they built Raeburn Road School which then became Raeburn Junior and Infant mixed. When they actually finished Raeburn Road School they moved us back into the junior part of it for a few years and then we were transferred back to the senior school which was a secondary modern school which was in Collingwood Drive again, so we went back to the old school.

I can remember them building Raeburn Road School putting the scaffolding up, the steel work. I remember at one stage an accident at the bottom of our garden in the actual building site where a dumper driver tipped up. I don't think he was badly injured, but that was something we remembered. A dumper tipped over and there was a lot of flapping around. I remember things like that happening and watching the thing being built, an iron railing fencing went all round the perimeter which ended up as our boundary fence.

Q. So all your education took place on Pheasey?

I stayed on the estate yes. We were almost like a small village most people knew each other on the estate because they were moving in when it was built like a new estate I suppose. Youngsters grew up and we all went to the same school, 'cause where you have two or three junior schools on the same estate now, then you only had one and we all moved up from the infants school up to the junior school. ... We had the same teacher for years and she moved with us from there when the junior school went across to Collingwood Drive and then when they finished Raeburn Road back to there and she retired. Her name was Mrs. Millington.

Q. How many classes were there in the school?

Oh, if there was four.

Q. One for each year?

Possibly something like that, it was very basic compared to what infants or primary schools are today we used to call it the infants school. I can remember as a youngster when it was my birthday having to stand, and I was so embarrassed, stand on a desk wile everyone sang happy birthday to me, but the teacher this Mrs. Millington was some sort of figure of authority, she was a lovely lady and she was the first woman in the area to have a television set. In fact we all went and watched the coronation on her television set now that was the sort of area it was, she invited you to her house for tea that sort of thing.

Old Hall Farm, 1950's

AT PLAY

We didn't go down around the Old Horns or over onto what used to be Park Farm side. We used to stay up here.

Q. Why was that?

I don't know, it just happened, one of these sort of things, we lived around Pomeroy and that way we had the sand pits that were virtually opposite us. Then we made a full size cycle track we had all got these racing bikes and we were able to ride these two wheeler things and we used to turn the handle bars up the other way and we used to have these race trials around these oval tracks that we built. And we had the sand pits ... there was no restriction we could go anywhere even to where Doe Bank playing fields were which wasn't a playing field then just a load of trees, the trees from here to over there just matched all together. We played at this end we had a rival group from Kingstanding used to come over here and it was always the Kingstanding and the Pheasey mob, I think it still exists. All they used to do they used to come over here and throw stones at us and we'd throw stones at them and they'd go or we'd go and that was it. That was as violent as anybody really got, fisticuffs and that sort of thing, but nobody was ever carted off to hospital and there was no big police enquiry and that sort of thing, didn't get that far. Although it was the Kingstanding mob are coming again and everyone was out in the fields waiting to see who was going to poke their head round a bush first, but we didn't go down to the bottom half of the estate, very rarely.

The bus service gradually improved. Originally I think we walked from Kingstanding Circle, then we got a bus across to The Trees on the Queslett Road, and then it came over up on to the Pheasey.

At one stage we had to pay an extra penny or tuppence to come up from across the Birmingham boundary come up to the bus terminus up here, I remember that.

They put a caravan there, and it was turned into a small cafe, all the bus drivers used to stop there and have a cup of tea when they were turning round because they used to have the old clock.

Q. The timing clock?

Yes as youngsters we used to love to go down the terminus because there were these bars we used to swing on, it wasn't a bus station or anything just an open space with these railings that we used swing on. And when the buses used to come we would say 'would you key us mate' and when they put the key into the clock it used to register on a piece of paper inside their number, and of course the ink was on the key and you used to put the key on your finger and you used to get as many of these as you could. That was your entertainment though there was nothing else.

That was what we used to do, we were teenagers we'd say can you key us mate and put your hand down and he'd say oh come on here ... We used to think that was fantastic. The café ended up selling all these penny and halfpenny sweets and things like this and we used to get a bag of sweets for about three ha'pence or threepence and take them into school.

At the back of the school you had the Old Barn and every Monday night they had a film night and one of the local fathers used to bring a projector up there, he'd got this sound projector and we used to go as youngsters and pay sixpence and watch the films. All the cowboy films and all that sort of thing and that was on a Monday night and on a Friday night we had a dance which was to records. ...

PHEASEY CINEMA SHOWS

Children ...... Monday, 6 p.m.

Children ...... Tuesday, 6 p.m.

Adults ...... Tuesday, 8.30 p.m.

IN THE OLD BARN

There wasn't any entertainment or anything on the estate you obviously had to make your own entertainment. All we had was what we called the Old Barn which had a cinema club and that was our Community Centre as such. It was three quarters of an hour by bus into Birmingham not like twenty minutes now and it was a long way to go. We very rarely went into Walsall although a lot of us on this side of the Queslett Road regarded Walsall as our town. If we said we were going to town we were going to Birmingham. My Dad used to go to the Villa. If anybody went anywhere it was always the Villa from up here.

Because again the buses went that way you see, I think what it was, most people that came to Pheasey had originally come from Birmingham I don't think there were many Pheasey people who came from Walsall when Pheasey was built.

Next to the Old Horns itself there were the cottages and there was a little shop and a blacksmiths. I had my first job I was a paper boy with Moreton's ... it was like a village shop when you went in. They came out of the back of the shop, which was their living room, they used to come out to serve you and it was an old oak counter and he always had a cigarette in his mouth. And you used to literally step down from the road into the shop at a slightly lower level.

Junction of Queslett Road and Barr Beacon, 1954

'Cause if you remember the Old Horns, the West Bromwich bus used to stop there and where the bay windows were you used to stand in and it was part of the tarmac of the old road, there was no pavement as such ... and when I worked for him I remember one of the paper boys got himself killed on the main road, on the Queslett Road on his bike ... Then the other paper shop was Richards who owned these shops round here which was at the Deers Leap and I did some paper work for him for a long time and that was when they were building this part of the estate. We used to get sixpence for every new paper account we got and we used to go mad, because they were building this new estate and this was my patch round here and it was great, I'd be knocking on the door, can we deliver your papers please. After about a month he gave us sixpence for that. 'Cause we were watching the place going up as well and seeing new houses and the new people moving in. Those were the only shops that we had up here and Park Farm wasn't built then, so there was nothing over that side.
Then they built the shops on the corner of Beacon Road and Queslett Road and we had Hewits the greengrocers and Gills the grocers which became Moyle and Adams and we had the post office, Mr. Barker.
And then we had believe it or believe it not, why on earth they had it there but when I think about it perhaps it catered for the people who were going to Barr Beacon, we had a milk bar, the Tartan Milk Bar.

In the 1950's and 1960's Birchfield Harriers of Perry Barr used this area for their cross country courses.

We ran a Midland up in Park Farm when George Smith was still farming and there was no Park Farm Estate, we ran a Midland Championship there. I ran in that myself. Birchfield won it and in 1952 we actually ran an English Championship over our course at Barr Beacon. That started on a field stretching from Beacon Road down to the bottom of the hill from Doe Bank Lane. ... You know it was a wonderful sight as they swept up the hill, there was a policeman on horseback clearing the spectators away --- it was about a three mile circuit, so they did three of them.
Q. Was it a good course?
It was a good course, but it was very stony ... we did try and find cart-tracks that were suitable, otherwise it was good, it was undulating and testing. ....
Q. Did you ever get any celebrities running on the course?
Oh, yes, the great Jack Holden who was well known, Gordon Pirie, and we have had all the Midland champions.

Queslett Road formed the boundary between the neighbouring authorities of Birmingham and Aldridge. Children from families living on the Birmingham side mostly attended schools belonging to that authority and did not have much opportunity for mixing with those on Pheasey until they became older. The boundary had implications regarding services such as post, police, fire, ambulance etc which was provided by each authority for its own area. Pheasey families had their bread delivered by Walsall Co-operative Society and those living on the Birmingham side of Queslett Road by Birmingham Co-op, they each served to their respective boundaries.

It was always a tale on the estate nobody ever proved it true, but the story was if someone had an accident on the Queslett Road it all depended which side of the white line he was lying on, that was the rumour because we were on a boundary. It was always strange no-one ever proved it was any different, but that was always the tale, oh if you had an accident on the Queslett Road, if you were on the Staffordshire side you went to Walsall now if it was on the other side you went to somewhere in Birmingham. All sorts of tales used to go around, like you'd get two fire engines facing each other on the Queslett Road saying well where's the fire, your side or mine? I don't think it ever happened but those were the tales that used to go around.

The Old Barn, at the rear of Collingwood Drive school, which years ago used to hold supplies of seed potatoes and corn when part of Pheasey Farm, was used as the Community Centre for Pheasey.

The Old Barn, 1949

Q. Can you tell me something about the Old Barn Community Association, what used to go on down there?
Well they used to have a kitchen club, gardening club, fishing club, darts club, billiards, dancing and they used to put on little concerts among the group, anybody would get up and do their party piece. There was tea and coffee in there and sandwiches but never anything alcoholic like you know...
Q. Was this a policy of First National Housing, that they didn't want alcohol there?
I don't know, but I never saw any all the years that I went there. And then they'd got this holiday bungalow at Barmouth that people could go to for a week which was a pound. We went on the tandem and it cost us a pound for a week to rent it... during the war this was and it was a lovely bungalow.

You got to Barmouth and you went over the railway lines over the level crossing and it belonged to Henry Boot & Sons and the Community shall I say as well. We went and we had a lovely holiday there for a pound for a week, you couldn't go for longer than a week because other people wanted to go. ... And with the families with young children it was easy to get on the train to go to Barmouth it was a lot cheaper than what it is today.
At the Old Barn they used to have games for the children, like a club night for the children and now what else did they have there? There was no Scout group or anything like that during the war. If anyone wanted to go out anywhere that was the place they went to, they'd got to walk there and walk back wherever it was, so it was the nearest place on your doorstep to go. We have had some great times there, there are quite a few of the old ones that I still know, 'cause most of them have popped off.
Q. What had you used to go down for yourself, what were you involved in?
My husband used to teach dancing, used to have a little dancing class you know 'cause we were dancing fanatics 'cause we have got our medals. We started one and all the teenagers used to come in you know.
Q. What sort of dancing was it they used to do then?
Ballroom, and all the latest dances and that, the Lambeth Walk and the Palais Glide ... but they used to enjoy it. But anybody who wanted to hold a birthday party or a party of any kind they could have the room, hire it for a few shillings in old money.

In January 1949 the Old Barn re-opened after extensive alterations costing £1,500. The concert hall now seated 180 people and in addition to a billiards room there was a common room suitable for small group meetings. The opening ceremony was performed by the chairman of the association Mr. G. Smith and he expressed the hope that all who entered the premises would receive social or educational benefit.

When they decided to set up this Community Association they decided that they would contribute two pence per week out of every household.

Q. Who decided that?
Oh they did, Mr. Boot, Charlie, a penny was used to run the Community Association and then a penny was put into a reserve fund and of course everybody thought that they were paying it, well I don't doubt in my own mind they were quite correct and they were paying it, but of course the great difference is this First National Housing Trust gave the tuppence you didn't pay it. They gave it even though you might have paid for it. And after the war years of course what we tried to do particularly when we set up our new Community Centre we tried to get the reserve fund which stood at just over £3,000 and we had quite a long long tussle to get it.

In 1959 Pheasey Community Association entered into discussions with Aldridge UDC about the future of the association as their present temporary accommodation was soon to be vacated. The Old Barn was demolished in the early 1960's when the site of a new centre was still undecided. It was several years before the new premises of Pheasey Park Farm Community Association were built in Hillingford Avenue.

HOUSES

The Pheasey houses, which were painted either green and cream or brown and cream, were built specifically for rental. Three rent collectors were employed by the Trust to collect each week and it was also part of their job to pass on any maintenance problems the tenants may have had if they couldn't get to the office themselves.

I will say this for First National Housing Trust, a lot of people wouldn't have agreed with me going back into late 1939, 40's I always found they were very good landlords. You could go over to the office and our office was in what was called the Old Barn complex and there was a house that had actually been the farmhouse originally which were then the offices of First National. You'd go over and give a complaint in to the fellow there you see and either the same day or sometime somebody would come round.

Q. When did you start to be the rent collector for First National?
It was about 1946 I started to become a rent collector and it was because one of the other rent collectors said do you want a job?... I went and saw Nellie Smith and she said oh I think you are capable of doing it. So I started rent collecting for £2.10.0. in old money a week.
Well you used to start out on a Monday and I used to do Hillingford Avenue, Greenaway Close, Cotman Close, Beacon Road, Drummond Road, Wimperis Way, that was my Monday mornings work. In the afternoon I used to do Tyndale from one end of Tyndale to the other, both sides I used to do, including Farrier and Crome. Then on a Wednesday I used to go round into Collingwood Drive, both sides, Raeburn Road and Pomeroy Road and that was that, and then you used to do your call books on a Wednesday all over and every dinner time you'd take your money back to

the farm to Boot's offices ... and you'd just be left with the change to go out again.

Q. So if people had got any complaints about the property did you have to deal with that as well?

Yes you used to have to take complaints, if the windows let in or the bricks were falling out anything like that, anything in general to the house like. And if they had garages built on to the side you used to have to report it.

On a Thursday, I used to get on my bike and ride up the Aldridge Road which was only a lane to the White house off Thornbridge Avenue and we used to balance all the books there, and at the back of there was all orchards it was beautiful that White house was.

Q. How many types of houses were there approximately do you recall?

There was the corner houses, which you'd got space for garages and there was the two bedroomed houses and three bedroomed, they'd all only got three bedrooms even the bigger houses, they were all built the same but some had got more ground than others. ...

Henry Boot built two houses in Crome Road that differed from the rest in their construction. During the years 1924-1930, Boot's built over 800 concrete houses by the 'Boot Pier and Panel Continuous Cavity System', these were erected on sites throughout the country and possibly these two at Pheasey were this type.

Well they were concrete throughout no wooden floors, ceilings or anything, they were absolutely solid concrete. We tried to get gas central fitted into them and although Boot's office was there and we told the Gas Board they could see the plans they said there would be no difficulty getting through. So after breaking no end of drills and puncturing the water supply they gave up.

In the early 1960's the rented houses were offered for sale en bloc by First National Housing Trust. The asking price included all fees and was seen as a very good deal made by the Trust. Banner Building Society had been set up and those who decided to buy their own house simply transferred to paying an amount which became a mortgage repayment instead of rent. Some people viewed the prospects of being a house owner with caution and were worried about the responsibility associated with ownership, others opted to carry on renting.

There was a big panic on the estate at the time. It was the year we got married so it was 1963 all of a sudden everybody was offered, did they want to buy their house. The re-action on the estate was terrific actually a lot of people panicked because rumours went round, if you don't buy it then somebody will buy it and you will be thrown out, which wasn't true.

The rent was converted into a mortgage it was a sort of progressive thing. It was good, because most of the people that did it were ten feet taller afterwards.

It took the likes of our age we were 21 then ... to tell our parents what to do because they weren't used to it, they were all frightened and I know we had a job to persuade my dad to buy it which he could then see the logic of it after a while. But my friend who lived four doors down her parents never bought theirs and they've since tried to buy it and couldn't.

GOING TO CHURCH

There were no permanent places of worship on Pheasey until after the war. However, temporary accommodation on the estate was soon arranged by the Anglican, Methodist and Evangelical churches.

> ... there was no church in the area so one or two Christians got together and met in a house, to start the church as it was, but that was the beginning they had absolutely nowhere else to meet.

In 1939 the Methodist Church started as a house fellowship in Tyndale Crescent and in 1940 moved to a wooden hut in Crome Road. A plot of land in Romney Way was donated to the church by Henry Boot in 1947 and the wooden hut was moved there from Crome Road and another added alongside. These huts remained in use as a place of worship until the 1950's when, due to the number of organisations and meetings, it became necessary to have larger premises. In 1954 plans were drawn up for a new brick church, manse, hall and other facilities. Money for this was made available by the Methodist authorities from compensation received for a church at Rocky Lane, Nechells which had been bombed during the war and other monies found by fundraising. A large charred cross from here was given to the new Pheasey Methodist Church which opened in 1957. The huts continued to give good service and were used regularly by the Brotherhood and Boys Brigade until the 1980's.

The temporary Methodist Church which has served Pheasey Estate since its earliest days. It is to be replaced by a permanent building of modern design costing over £31,000. Contracts for the new building will be placed within the next few weeks.

The temporary Methodist Church, 1954

The first Anglican services were held in the Barn during the Autumn of 1941. At this time Pheasey was part of Great Barr Parish and the services were mostly taken by Rev. J. Reaney father of the present vicar. When the estate was first planned a site was set aside for a church on the corner of Collingwood Drive and Hillingford Avenue but the outbreak of war prevented any developments during that period. A temporary building was found for a church in 1947. It was the first of its kind to be erected in the Lichfield Diocese since the end of the war combining a church and a hall. The former Y.M.C.A. hut which had served on an RAF station in some other part of the country was bought to Pheasey in sections and re-erected. The Chancel was an annexe which could be closed off from the remainder of the hall by sliding doors. The hall had a small stage and numerous social events were held in this temporary church which was dedicated to St. Chad on 22 March 1947 by the Bishop of Lichfield.

> It was 1947 before we got our temporary building for the church up the road. It was like an old Y.M.C.A. hut and they made an extension on the end for the sanctuary, and they had doors that drew across and you turned all the chairs around and there was a stage on the other end of the room that you could have concerts and that sort of thing.
> In July 1961 the Reverend D. Bishop was licensed by the Bishop of Lichfield with sole responsibility to St. Chad's church. Mr. Bishop was a qualified architect and plans were now formulated for the building of a permanent church. The Parsonage house was already built in 1953 on the site of the new church.
> The Bishop of Lichfield consecrated the church of St. Chad's on the 24 October 1964 - actually the people of St. Margaret's helped us to build the church, we were a daughter church because the vicar used to come over and take services.

The nearest Evangelical Church was at Kingstanding and their first services to be held on Pheasey were in the Old Barn Community Centre and the Sunday School which catered for a lot of children was in a house on Queslett Road.

Dedication of the Evangelical Church site in Romney Way, July 1954

I have still got my first prize upstairs I went there first in someone's house and I can remember we used to sit on the table, in the sink, and that was the Sunday School. They didn't actually have the church they still went to the church in Kingstanding but because there were so many children up here and no Sunday School as such they opened up this Sunday School in their own home and that's where the church grew from.

My parents were Church of England but there again the nearest church on the Birmingham side was Perry Beeches which was St. Matthew's which is where I was actually christened. It was too far to go for them because there were no buses or cars, and they wanted me to go to Sunday School so they sent me to this ladies house. But obviously it was a different kind of church to what they were used to. When I got into my teens and wanted to belong to the church, the church actually practices baptism by full immersion, and I always remember asking my dad if I could become baptised and he said but you've been baptised as a child and we explained everything to him and he agreed and I became an actual member of the church, because you became a member if you are actually baptised into the church.

The senior members of the church decided they should have their own place of worship on Pheasey however they were then faced with the enormous problems of finance and locating a plot of ground. After two or three years land was eventually obtained from Aldridge UDC, this was some of the vacant area at the rear of The Trees public house which had been sold back to the Council by the brewery following their decision not to develop the plot into tennis courts and a bowling green. So with great courage they then set about building their church themselves.

Laying the foundations, August 1955

So eventually I joined them hoping that along with others I could influence them to forget all about a temporary building. I felt it would be more commendable to start off with some sort of permanent building but I realised at the same time that due to the financial situation we would have to build it ourselves to save money.
We tried for two or three years but all the ground was owned either by the First National Housing Trust, The Aldridge Council or the breweries.

Because there was no entertainment or anything, the church, the Evangelical Church that we belonged to was very youth orientated they used to bring the young people together and we met there and we spent our courtship there. We used to meet as a church in the Old Barn or in one of the school rooms for mid-week meetings and we were part of the building we spent our courtship actually building it because Pheasey Evangelical Church was actually built by the people who owned the church it wasn't built by builders.
Q. So what did you actually do then?
Well I was the tea girl.

The older members in the church took courses on building in concrete and electrical courses but as I say they would be in their thirties or forties you see then and we were sort of in our teens. And if we needed everybody to dig out a trench they'd give you a shovel and we all got in and had a great time doing it. On a Saturday we'd have tea there round a big table and everybody would bring sandwiches or the ladies would do sandwiches. ... used to make the tea in the tea hut all day long. We had got an old concrete mixer none of these ready mix lorries, a concrete mixer, the lads used to shovel all the mixes into buckets and throw them into the mixer for the older ones to turn the handle and tip it out. Somebody was up a ladder, we did that every Saturday and every Wednesday night plus all the other things for the church. Worship services they used to be held in the Old Barn on a Sunday.

Helping Hands, August 1959

The Erdington News reported on their progress in 1959 and quoted the secretary of the building committee, Mr. A. Ridpath, as saying 'before we could think of building we had to get a wheelbarrow and move over 300 tons of rubble and top soil'. The reporter was obviously impressed by the expert way the workers tackled their jobs.

> Q. Perhaps if you could tell me something of the organisation of getting people working - who was in charge, did you have teams doing different things?
>
> When I came to assess what labour we had got and the qualifications, we hadn't got a bricklayer. Now before we started this project I visited a number of churches that had built their own in Birmingham or Birmingham area and they were really amateurish, you can't get away from it, good bricklaying is professional it's got to be, and there's nothing I like better than a good brick building but when you haven't got skilled people it is just hopeless. I felt the only answer was to build it in concrete. I decided that the best thing I could do was to take a two year evening course during the winter months at what was Suffolk Street Building Technical School, it's all been demolished now. I took a two year course in concrete technology so as to get a grip of concrete making and so on. We had got one or two engineers amongst us and I have said a good engineer should be able to put his hand to anything.
>
> It worked, and I had to sort out, to allocate jobs, I had to sort out because we had got some very willing but terribly ham fisted ... one thing, I did learn this, you have to plan and prepare so that whoever comes up you can give them a job because if they come up and you don't give 'em anything we won't see them again.

Children were keen to help too and families gave up their weekends to assist with the latest stage of the building.

> ... We catered for them, so that the parents would come knowing that the children had got something to do. We had got a big load of sand and they used to play sand castles. During one summer main holiday week in Birmingham, it was very hot and some of the workers improvised a large tarpaulin supported and filled with water and you'd see the kiddies paddling in it in their swimming suits. Now sometimes when we'd got a big project on we'd put a couple of hours in before breakfast and some of the ladies would come along and get breakfast for us. We've had supper up there when we have been working very late because we had got to get a project done.

Work started in the summer of 1954 and the project was completed in 1962. During this time 465 tons of concrete were used in the construction of the building, which in those days cost 5 shillings a bag. Also several hundred tons of soil and rubble were moved and probably hundreds of gallons of tea consumed by the workforce. The total cost of the actual building was £3,500 which worked out at about £10 a week for materials only, the labour being free.

> When we had the official opening with both buildings completed we weren't in debt.

The completed project, 1962

Coronation Day preparations in Cattermole Grove, 1953

CORONATION DAY JUNE 1953

Plans on the estate to celebrate Coronation Day were well underway almost twelve months before the event. Collections were organised in every street and in Chantrey Crescent notice boards were placed outside the houses of the street committee to inform all the residents of the present level of funds. One shilling a week had been paid by households since the previous July. It was planned to have souvenirs for all the children, a fancy dress parade, sports and an impressive tea. Housewives made plenty of street decorations in red, white and blue.

This was very much the scene all across Pheasey, in Gainsborough Crescent there were 34 children from 22 houses and husbands had promised to level off a nearby field for sports. Residents of Cattermole Grove put forward ideas to landscape their traffic island by planting bushes and turfing the edges.

On Coronation Day the weather was unkind with wind and rain, but this failed to put off nearly 3,000 spectators from climbing Barr Beacon to witness the lighting of a bonfire which was one of the links in a chain of beacons across the country. Cars were lined up three and four deep and at 10.30 p.m. a rocket was fired by the scouts to signify that the fire was about to be lit. Alderman E.J. Denton used a flaming torch to start the paraffin soaked brushwood and as the flames shot skywards the royal cipher was illuminated in red, white and blue.

It had taken six men nearly three days to build the bonfire, the timber was provided by Walsall Corporation and the brushwood by Aldridge UDC. A spokesperson from Aldridge claimed it was one of the biggest if not the biggest bonfire ever to be held on the Beacon. It was 20 feet high and 60 yards round and contained approximately 200 cubic yards of wood and rubbish. The illuminated royal ciphers on 30 foot high scaffolding were to have been in neon lighting but on the day before the Coronation strong winds had blown it down. Ten employees from the Truman Electrical Co. in Walsall had worked almost non-stop to rebuild the scaffolding and wire up coloured bulbs.

After the bonfire had been lit a new topograph plate was unveiled by Mr. C.A. Bragg, a great nephew of Colonel J.H. Wilkinson the donor of the memorial and Barr Beacon itself for the benefit of the public in 1919. The plate was then taken away for final enamelling.

Farm below Barr Beacon

Pheasey was created by private enterprise at a time when renting accommodation was the normal practice amongst the working class. The aim of the builders was to provide good homes at an economical rent in areas where there was the greatest demand for homes. As building land in the City of Birmingham was becoming difficult to obtain Pheasey was seen as a good option. Development was halted by the war years and resumed as soon as restrictions on building were lifted. Initially a young estate with families growing up together and creating their own community it has now become an established suburb with most homes owner-occupied and the elderly specially catered for in purpose-built flats.

I think it is a better and more settled estate now ... they are doing up their houses and staying put so it is ageing rather than it used to be with a continual influx of younger people.

During the course of research for this book information came to light which has not been included in the text. The following is a short list derived from minutes of Aldridge UDC, newspaper articles etc.

4.6.1941	Emergency Comm.	Request for permission for First Aid Post.
20.3.1942	Birmingham Mail	Report of Pioneers at a Midland camp on an 'immense housing estate, a miniature Aldershot'.
15.7.1942	Emergency Comm.	Fireguards at Pheasey were compulsorily enrolled into the Home Guard.
12.9.1942	Walsall Observer	Army Cadets in manoeuvres on Barr Beacon.
10.1.1948	" "	Local councillors plea for better lighting at Pheasey.
14.8.1948	" "	Five bands accompany Pheasey's Carnival Queen, over 4,000 people at Community Fete. This the second annual carnival by the 'small but progressive community'. Prize for best front garden won by Mr. Yardley of Beacon Road.
13.5.1950	" "	'Coal Found This Week At Barr Beacon' a thick seam possibly 30 feet found at a depth of 2,300 feet at a test site in Crook Lane. In 1948 borings at Queslett Road struck a similar seam.
2.8.1950	" "	Report of Pheasey Garden Guild's show held at the Old Barn.
16.9.1950	" "	Garden of Memory at St. Chad's dedicated to the fallen of both World Wars.
16.6.1951	" "	George Smith crowns Carnival Queen as part of Festival of Britain celebration. Other activities included an exhibition of boxing and square dancing.
1.9.1951	" "	New Beacon reservoir nearly completed, capacity 10,000,000 gallons.
15.10.1951	Acorn to Oak	New Pheasey branch of the Co-op opened by Councillor Mrs. F.E. Davies J.P. the society claimed that this shop was the most hygienic grocery and provisions store in the county.
6.2.1952	Walsall Observer	Street committees all over Pheasey collecting to provide parties for children on Coronation Day.
30.4.1954	" "	New topograph unveiled on Barr Beacon.
6.7.1954	" "	Corner of Queslett Road and Beacon Road described as a 'real death trap' due to there being no footpath.
11.2.1955	" "	Extra bus for children attending school at Pheasey.
1.4.1955	" "	Plans for improvements to roads, footpaths and lighting and also shops in Bonnington Square.

Date	Source	Event
14.4.1955	General Purposes Committee Aldridge UDC	Branch Library at Pheasey now under jurisdiction of Aldridge Library Committee; the voluntary librarian has been replaced by library assistants.
3.6.1955	Walsall Observer	Barr Beacon crowded over the holiday weekend and parking arrangements were found to be totally inadequate.
16.6.1955	General Purposes Committee Aldridge UDC	Aldridge Library Committee had inspected the existing library facilities at Pheasey and decided to recommend to the committee that better accommodation and books should be provided. Clerk to approach First National Housing Trust for a short term lease of land at the corner of Hillingford Avenue and Collingwood Drive and a hut is to be provided.
1.7.1955	Walsall Observer	Topograph on the Beacon damaged by vandals.
13.2.1958	General Purposes Committee Aldridge UDC	Ministry of Housing and Local Government give approval in principle for construction of new branch library and it was anticipated that work would begin in the current year.
30.6.1958	Walsall Observer	Evangelical rally on Barr Beacon organised by Birmingham Youth Rallies.
15.2.1959	Housing Committe Aldridge UDC	Application from Henry Boot & Sons Ltd proposing 72 houses for Hillingford Avenue, Gainsborough Crescent, Cooksey Close and Romney Way.
3.5.1959	Sunday Mercury	Death of Jesse Williams, well known Pheasey man who had helped many with their legal problems.
6.5.1959	Housing Committee Aldridge UDC	Resolved. Decision not to acquire further land at Pheasey for general council housing. F.N.H.T. confirmed decision not to sell land at Pheasey for local authority housing other than aged persons scheme.
14.5.1959	General Purposes Committee Aldridge UDC	Post Office authorised at Deers Leap
9.3.1960	Planning Committee Aldridge UDC	Parks Superintendant reported that 2,500 circulars had been distributed at Pheasey and only 55 requests had been made for allotment tenancies. It was suggested that arable land owned by the Council at the junction of Beacon Road and Wimperis Way would be suitable for the allotments.
29.3.1961	Parks & Allotments Committee Aldridge UDC	48 Allotments had been marked and pegged out and it was anticipated that 10 plots would be taken up shortly.
26.5.1961	Walsall Observer	Pheasey will fight hard to remain in Aldridge and oppose new boundary proposals to include them with Birmingham.

12.9.1962	General Purposes Committee Aldridge UDC	Pheasey Horticultural Society congratulated on a display at local show.
29.11.1962	Planning Committee Aldridge UDC	Application approved for the rebuilding of The Old Horns public house on land at the rear of existing property. The committee expressed hope that anything of historical or architectural interest found in the old building be kept.
6.12.1962	Health Committee Aldridge UDC	Clean Air Act 1956 - order confirmed for Pheasey and Park Farm estates to come into force 1.7.1963
23.10.1963	Walsall Observer	Infant Welfare Centre opens at Pheasey.
24.1.1964	Planning Committee Aldridge UDC	Henry Boot & Sons Ltd, application for erection of 2 storey office block on land at the north end of Crome Road.
7.8.1964	Walsall Observer	Old Horns public house closes for demolition.
21.6.1966	" "	Doe Bank County Primary Infants & Junior School opened by Sir Alfred Owen.